To Donna & Dale,

Merry Christmas, 1992.

May you enjoy many Christmas' in your new LOG CABIN!

Love,

Jeanne

Beautiful America's

Wyoming

Published by Beautiful America Publishing Company
9725 S.W. Commerce Circle
Wilsonville, Oregon 97070

Library of Congress Cataloging in Publication Data
Beautiful America's Wyoming
1. Wyoming — Description and travel — Views.
I. Beautiful America (Firm)   II. Title.   III. Title: Wyoming.
F762.D59   1989   917.41—dc20   89-6519
ISBN 0-89802-539-7
ISBN 0-89802-538-9 (Paperback)

Old Faithful

Beautiful America's

Wyoming

Text by
Charlotte Dixon

Table of Contents

Introduction

Wyoming. Mention the name of this vast western state and what image springs to mind? Perhaps it's a vision of Yellowstone National Park, or maybe it's cowboys, or Indians. Possibly you'd think of oil fields and coal mines. At one time or another any of these images could have served as a fitting symbol for the story of Wyoming.

There is one element, however, which ties these disparate pictures together: the land. Because, throughout Wyoming's history, it is the land which has shaped the state's fortunes, and it is the land which shapes Wyoming's story today.

It's easy to see why. Covering an area of nearly 100,000 square miles, and inhabited by just over 400,000 people, Wyoming is indeed a region ruled by a close relationship to the landscape. This is, after all, the homeland of the great Plains Indians, the tribes of the Shoshone, Arapaho and Crow, who shared the territory's wide open spaces with great herds of buffalo and an amazing abundance of wildlife. To the Indian, the land was sacred.

And this, too, is the land of the fur trapper. Jim Bridger, Jacques LaRamie and David Jackson were among the first white men to view the area. Their stalwart explorations paved

Granite Mountains along Oregon Trail

Sierra Madre Mountains in Continental Divide (Opposite

the way for future generations.

This is the land which countless pioneers labored across, their numbers so plentiful and wagons so laden that they etched permanent ruts into the earth. Major interstate highways today replace the dusty trails the emigrants followed, but their legacy of hope remains.

And, yes, this is the land of the Wild West, where Buffalo Bill Cody once reigned supreme, and his kindred spirit, the cowboy, still does.

So it is fitting to speak first of the geography of this sometimes unruly land. It is a state of contrast and variety. Towering mountain ranges, deep canyons, and dry, dusty plains alternate with forested areas. The scenic wonders and thermal features of Yellowstone caused it to be designated the country's first national park. Together with its neighbor to the south, Grand Teton National Park, Yellowstone attracts millions of visitors each summer.

There are other firsts in Wyoming. Devil's Tower in the state's northeastern corner was the first national monument. The Shoshone National Forest in northwestern Wyoming was the first timberland to be so designated. Seven additional national forests now lie wholly or partially in Wyoming. Combine them with two national recreation areas, 10 state parks, a national elk refuge, a national grassland and numerous historic sites, and you've got a state which is replete with areas set aside for the benefit of the public.

With an average elevation of 6,100 feet, and an average rainfall of just 14.5 inches, most of the state is designated, "semi-arid." Though farming is important, in much of Wyoming the soil is unsatisfactory, with a mere eight percent of the land having ever been plowed. Major cash crops are hay, wheat, sugar beets and barley.

Mining, cattle ranching and tourism are of primary importance to the economy. Oil is the biggest contributor to the state's coffers, and 50 percent of the Rocky Mountain region's crude comes from Wyoming fields. And, with 19 million acres of workable coal seams, Wyoming leads all other states in coal reserves.

As for ranching, more than one million head of cattle are raised in the state, and a similar number of sheep are reared, placing Wyoming just third behind Texas and California in wool production.

And, then, there's the wildlife. The state is an animal watcher's dream. Its diverse geography has given rise to an enormous diversity of species. More than 100 varieties of mammals alone roam the wilds of Wyoming, including pronghorn antelope, bison, deer, elk, moose, bighorn sheep, and, of course, the bear. Add to that 340 species of birds and 78 species of fish and it's safe to say that animals are far more abundant than people in Wyoming.

History buffs will find much to interest them here. Museums dot the state, as do historic sites such as Fort Laramie, Fort Bridger, and Independence Rock. Monuments, memorials, and markers help to explain Wyoming's colorful history, which has all the elements of a classic Western tale. This was the territory where Butch Cassidy and his "Wild Bunch" roamed, where cattle rustlers and stagecoach robbers worked, where Indians and white men alike were massacred in continuing disputes.

This Wild West history is celebrated in festivals around the state. Fort Fetterman Days are held near Douglas, or try the Green River Rendezvous Pageant in Pinedale, to name only a couple. Indian culture is observed with Sun Dances on the Wind River Indian Reservation, the Laubin Ancient Indian Dances at Jackson, and The Gift of the Waters Pageant in Thermopolis.

But the story of Wyoming is not all wild derring-do. This land which required its occupants to be tough and hardy also fostered an unusual fair-mindedness. It's for good reason that the state's nickname is "The Equality State," and that its motto is "Equal Rights." For it was here that women first earned the right to vote.

Legislation was passed by the territorial government in 1869 granting woman's suffrage, and when Wyoming became a state in 1890, the law was incorporated into the state's constitution. Wyoming can boast of the first woman justice of the peace, Esther Hobart

Officers Quarters at Fort Bridger State Historical Site

Old cabin near Encampment, looking to Medicine Bow Mountain

Morris, and the first woman governor, Nellie Tayloe Ross, who served from 1925 to 1927, and later became the first woman director of the U.S. Mint.

Wyoming celebrates its centennial in 1990, and there is much in its history and current affairs of which it can be proud. More importantly for our immediate purposes, there is much to do and see in this spectacular state. Let's get started on our tour!

The Wide Open Spaces:
Southern Wyoming

We begin our tour of the "Equality State" in southern Wyoming. Wagon train emigrants who chose the Overland Trail for their western journey witnessed the stark beauty of this landscape. Later, pioneers of a different sort, the railroad company workers, laid tracks across this region as the dream of a transcontinental railroad took shape. Many of the communities in the southern half of the state owe their existence to the coming of the railroad.

Today, the major highway Interstate 80 crosses southern Wyoming. (Would that those early pioneers had had such an easy, fast, route to follow!) First up is Cheyenne, Wyoming's state capital. It is named after the Indian tribe which lived in the area long before the white men came.

Known as "Hell on Wheels" in its early days, the town was incorporated in 1867, when the railroad arrived. Cattle barons and cowboys established ranches on the abundant grasslands which surround the city, and in its Old West heyday Cheyenne was a rollicking, bawdy headquarters for outlaws and upstanding citizens alike.

Lincoln Monument near Cheyenne

Mirror Lake, Sierra Madre Mountains (Opposite)

Historic South Pass City

15

Considerably calmer today, the city preserves this heritage with the famous Cheyenne Frontier Days. Events include western parades, chuck wagon races, and free chuck wagon breakfasts during which up to 100,000 pancakes have been known to be served. (Cement trucks are called in to mix up the batter!)

For a quieter change of pace, a visit to the Wyoming State Capitol may be just the antidote. The building's gold leaf dome dominates the city's skyline and offers visitors panoramic views. Its Corinthian architecture adds a classical note to this western city. In keeping with the state's motto, "Equal Rights," a statue of Esther Hobart Morris stands in front of the capitol. She was an outspoken proponent of woman's suffrage, and, fittingly, the first woman justice of the peace in the world.

Just a few minutes away from the capitol is the Wyoming State Museum, which houses a treasure trove of western memorabilia. Stop in, too, at the National First Day Cover Museum. Dedicated to the preservation and display of First Edition postage stamps, this unique museum boasts a collection valued at $750,000. And then there's the Cheyenne Frontier Days Old West Museum which features western artifacts relating to the festival's history from its first staging in 1897.

Railroad devotees will want to stop at Holliday Park. Here you'll view "Big Boy," the world's largest steam locomotive. Old Number 4004 was retired from duty in 1956 and moved to the park for public viewing. This old work horse did the job of two conventional steam engines, carrying 28 tons of fuel and 25,000 gallons of water as it plied a rugged stretch of track between Cheyenne and Ogden, Utah.

From Cheyenne, we'll head west to Laramie. The fastest way to get there is by I-80, but those in search of scenic vistas may opt for the "Happy Jack" Road, Route 210. This way passes out of rolling grasslands into mountain foothills, and soon the traveler is immersed in the Medicine Bow National Forest.

But wayfarers who choose to stick to I-80 have several sights to take in, too. Just 30 miles

Black Mountain near Lamont

west of Cheyenne is a 42½ foot bronze monument to President Abraham Lincoln, sculpted by Robert Russin. This memorial to the great president, whose dream of a transcontinental railroad was so instrumental in much of Wyoming's history, stands at the summit of Sherman Hill. At 8,640 feet, this was the highest point of the first railroad.

Next along our southern tour is Laramie, a city situated at an altitude of more than 7,000 feet. One of the first white men to travel in the area was French-Canadian fur trapper Jacques LaRamie, and he gave the town its name.

Within three months of the railroad's arrival in May of 1868, Laramie's population boomed to 5,000. In its early days Laramie was the site of two historic events which proved the territory's commitment to equality. The first woman in the world served on a court jury here in March of 1870, attracting national attention. A short time later, in the Fall of 1871, "Grandma" Louiza Swain became the first woman to vote in a general election.

Another early resident was lecturer and writer Bill Nye. He started the Laramie Boomerang, a newspaper named after his favorite mule, in the 1870's. It's been published daily ever since. Nye arrived in the area practically penniless, but thanks to the opportunities of the western boom town, he went on to become justice of the peace, U.S. Commissioner, editor, postmaster and correspondent for several regional newspapers.

Laramie today is home to the University of Wyoming, which was founded in 1886, four years before Wyoming became a state. The 780-acre campus features a geological museum, and anthropology museum, a fine arts center, and the Rocky Mountain Herbarium, all of interest to visitors.

We'll continue our path by heading west to Rawlins. But once again, journeyers face a choice. The options include I-80, of course, which along this stretch traces the path of the Overland Trail, a stagecoach and covered wagon route across the high Laramie Plains. Travelers along this route can see the ruins of Fort Fred Steele, an army post which operated from 1868 to 1886. It protected crews working on the Union Pacific Railroad from hostile Indians.

Heading out on U.S. 30, you'll pass through Rock River, a small town which changed its location and its name in order to keep pace with the railroad. This is premiere cowboy country, and it's also the site of the Como Bluff Dinosaur Graveyard and Museum, whose fossil beds have produced tons of dinosaur bones, supplying natural history museums worldwide. The museum building is constructed entirely of dinosaur bones, and can thus legitimately claim the title of "oldest building in America."

Further on along this course we arrive at Medicine Bow, the town made famous by the 1902 publication of Owen Wister's novel, *The Virginian*. When the author arrived in town in 1855, he was forced to sleep his first night in the general store, since a hotel wasn't built until 1911. Both the store and the hotel (named The Virginian, naturally) are town landmarks. Wister's famous book inspired two stage plays, two silent films, one "talkie," and a television series. The Medicine Bow Museum, located across from the hotel, shows the history of the area.

An alternate western route from Laramie is Highway 130, a road which passes through the Snowy Range Division of the Medicine Bow National Forest, a one-million acre timberland created by President Theodore Roosevelt in 1902. The road climbs to 12,000 feet as it traverses the Medicine Bow Mountains, known to locals as the "Snowy Range." Closed to snow in the winter, this pass affords views of several lakes, as well as the snow-capped mountains themselves.

Connecting Laramie with the resort town of Saratoga is Highway 230. Saratoga is known for its natural hot springs, whose waters average 114 degrees. On the way to Saratoga, you'll pass through Encampment, where huge gatherings of Indians converged to hunt buffalo and other game. From 1897 to 1908, a copper mining town was located here, but was deserted when the vein ran out. The Grand Encampment Museum features 14 ghost town

Vedauwoo Rock Formations near Laramie

Ferris Mountain in Great Basin Desert (Opposite)

buildings, including, believe it or not, a two-story outhouse! Memorabilia from the copper mining times and Indian encampment days is shown.

Rawlins was founded in 1868, when, you guessed it, the Union Pacific Railroad came through. Newly discovered gold mines fueled the town's importance as a departure point for wagon trains and stagecoaches. By the 1870's the community had gained a reputation as a wild place with a large population of outlaws. So citizens eager to salvage their town's pride took matters into their own hands, lynching "Big Nose" George Parrott and sending warnings to 24 of his cronies. They left town in a hurry the next morning. Today Rawlins is a center for the sheep and cattle raising industry. Coal, gas, and uranium are mined in the area, too.

West from Rawlins, we'll pass through a 108-mile stretch of desert land. This is the Red Desert, also know as "The Sands." It is a land of little rainfall and lots of wildlife, including one of the largest herds of wild horses in the country. Nearby Rock Springs is a mining and refining center. In its early days it was a way station on the Overland Stage route.

South of Rock Springs lies the Flaming Gorge National Recreation Area, 201,000 acres of land in southwestern Wyoming and eastern Utah. At its center is a 90-mile long reservoir. The Firehole Canyon region boasts especially unique rock formations and pinnacles, but the entire area is filled with interesting geological history. The compositions were caused by silt and mud build-up 40 million years ago when this was a vast fresh-water sea.

Past Rock Springs is the Fort Bridger State Historic Site. Established by famed mountain man Jim Bridger in 1843, it was second in importance only to Fort Laramie as an outfitting point for travelers on the Overland Trail. In 1853, however, it was taken over by Mormons, and the resulting "Mormon Wars" saw the burning of the fort by army troops in 1857. Rebuilt and officially designated a military outpost a year later, it also served as a station on the Pony Express and Overland Stage routes. The fort was closed in 1890.

Now, displays and interpretive features guide the visitor interested in western history. A museum displays artifacts, and some of the fort's original structures have been restored.

Evanston is the last stop on our southern Wyoming sojourn. Once known as Bear River, the town lies in the middle of the energy-rich Overthrust Belt and is the center for drilling operations for oil and gas companies.

And with that, we've finished our trek across southern Wyoming. Next we'll head up the western side of the state, where visits to two renowned national parks and much spectacular scenery await us.

Plume Rocks and Wind River Mountains

Badlands near Marbleton in Great Basin

The Natural Wonders:
Western Wyoming

Ah, Western Wyoming. The landscape here is one of unrivaled beauty and many natural wonders, including the thermal oddities of Yellowstone National Park and the awesome Grand Tetons. But that's getting ahead of the story.

Our initial stop is at Kemmerer. Coal veins discovered in 1897 assured the town's future growth. But the city's most famous resident staked his future not to the coal industry, but to a retail store. His name was J.C. Penney, and he opened his first store, named the Golden Rule, in Kemmerer in 1902. His home can be seen at 107 J.C. Penney Ave.

A bit west of Kemmerer is a fascinating, brightly colored badlands area, the Fossil Butte National Monument. The butte itself juts up 1,000 feet above the Twin Creek Valley. Here lies one of the world's largest deposits of fossilized fresh-water fish, that lived 50 million years ago. Also fossilized are insects, snails, clams, birds, bats and plants. Established as a national monument in 1972, Fossil Butte offers ranger-guided hikes as well as a two-and-a-half mile self-guided hiking trail. A visitor's center is open daily in summer.

Heading north from Kemmerer we'll pass two historical sites. On the Green River is the location of the Old Mormon Ferry, which was built in 1847 by Mormons on their way to the Great Salt Lake Valley. Further north is Names Hill, or the "Calendar of the West," where emigrants taking the Sublette Cutoff carved their names in the soft sandstone. Look for mountain man Jim Bridger's name among the hundreds of others etched here. This testament to pioneer fortitude is located a few miles south of La Barge.

One of western Wyoming's many natural phenomena is Periodic Spring, in the Bridger-Teton National Forest. The spring flows intermittently, ceasing every 18 minutes, then gradually building again to a torrent releasing large volumes of water. Nobody knows quite why this occurs, but it happens regularly for nine months of the year, stopping only during high water runoff times from May to August.

As for the land in which the spring is located, the Bridger-Teton National Forest is the result of a merger, in 1973, of the Bridger and Teton timberlands. This combination brought together three-and-a-half million acres and seven ranger districts under one jurisdiction. The state's highest point, Gannett Peak (13,804 feet), lies within its boundaries. So do several live glaciers, and numerous lakes. Just as you'd expect, recreation opportunities abound, with 500 miles of hiking trails in the Bridger division alone. Other activities include horseback trips, fishing, camping, and backpacking.

Near the forest's southern boundary are two monuments marking Wyoming's colorful history. The Upper Green River Rendezvous National Historic Landmark designates the environs where fur traders, mountain men, and Indians gathered from throughout the West to barter, sell, and, of course, raise hell. Every year in July, this gathering is reenacted in The Green River Rendezvous Pageant in Pinedale. Further west is the Father DeSmet Monument, commemorating the priest who celebrated the first mass in Wyoming on July 5, 1840.

But now it's time to head north into Jackson Hole Country. Rimmed by the Grand Teton Mountains, and bisected by the Snake River, Jackson Hole is a high mountain valley nearly

Continental Divide from Mount Wachakie

Sunrise on Cirque of the Towers, Shoshone National Forest (Opposite)

50 miles long and six to twelve miles wide. Fur trader David Jackson lent his name to this valley where wildlife, including such rarities as the trumpeter swan, roam.

The town of Jackson, situated at the southern end of the "hole" is noted for its western ambiance. It has long attracted artists, vacationers and outdoor enthusiasts. And it's no wonder why, for Jackson offers numerous attractions, museums, galleries and cultural events among them.

The Grand Teton Music Festival boasts world-class symphony concerts in summer. Come September, the Jackson Hole Fall Arts Festival is presented, confirming the area's reputation as a western arts center. But for a different sort of cultural experience, try the Jackson Hole Shootouts held summer evenings in the town square. You'll witness an Old West style robbery and capture.

Museums flourish here. More than 250 paintings and sculptures by well-known western artists are in The Wildlife of the American West Art Museum. Western history spanning the years from the fur-trading era to pioneer days is interpreted at the Jackson Hole Historical Museum. And, at Ross Berlin's Wildlife Museum, mounted big game animals are exhibited against the backdrop of murals depicting their natural habitats.

Those who prefer outdoor recreation can arrange for float trips on the Snake River with one of many companies headquartered in the area. Or, take a covered wagon trip into the back country for a taste of the life of a pioneer. The nearby Elk Refuge is the winter home to 7,500 elk, one of the largest herds in North America. In winter, you can take a sleigh ride to view them. When the elk shed their antlers in the spring, Boy Scouts collect them for auctioning in the town square.

And, of course, there is the skiing. The name Jackson Hole is practically synonymous with premiere skiing for devotees of the sport. Several first-rate resorts, including Grand Targhee and Teton Village are located here. Summertime visitors can ride the Jackson Hole Aerial Tram to the top of 10,450 foot Rendezvous Mountain for a panoramic view of

Jackson Hole and the Teton Range.

Though the temptations of Jackson could easily hold us longer, there is much more to explore as we head north. An interesting sidelight is the Gros Ventre Slide area near Kelly. On June 23, 1925, a huge earthen slide dammed up the Gros Ventre River in a lake five miles long. Two years later, the dam gave way and a wall of water, mud and rock destroyed the town of Kelly. A self-guided tour explains this natural phenomenon.

Breath-taking Grand Teton National Park actually includes most of Jackson Hole and much of the Teton Range. Within its 485-square mile boundaries are eight large lakes, many small ones, 12 glaciers, several snowfields and extensive forests. The park was established in 1929, but greatly enlarged in 1950.

Among the largest lakes are Jackson and Jenny. Jackson Lake covers almost 26,000 acres and is over 16 miles long. The Tetons rise majestically from the lake's western shore to a height of as much as 7,000 feet above the lake. Jenny Lake, the second largest in the park, lies at an elevation of 6,783 feet. It was named for a Shoshone Indian maiden who died tragically. She was the wife of Richard "Beaver Dick" Leigh, who gave his name to Leigh Lake.

The Colter Bay and Moose Visitor's Centers offer exhibits, information and interpretive displays. Over 200 miles of trails criss-cross the park, among them the Amphitheatre Lake Trail which passes two alpine lakes at the 9,000 foot elevation. Other recreation activities include fishing, boating, horseback riding, mountain climbing and float trips. Summer visitors to the park can watch the Laubin Ancient Indian Dances, held in July and August on Friday nights. They celebrate life of the American Indian before the white man arrived.

Heading further north, we'll travel via the John D. Rockefeller Memorial Parkway, dedicated in 1972 as a memorial to the man who donated the land which greatly enlarged Grand Teton National Park. He made numerous other contributions to the national park system.

Aspens in the fall

And then there is Yellowstone. Though devastating forest fires in the summer of 1988 have changed its look for decades to come, it's doubtful they'll have much impact on the park's popularity. Established in 1872, it was our first national park, one of the largest, (bigger than the states of Rhode Island and Delaware combined), and arguably, the best known. While parts of the park spill over into Montana and Idaho, most of its 3,472 square miles lie in Wyoming.

The park's attractions are numerous and diverse. It is perhaps most famous for its 10,000 thermal features, reports of which led to an early moniker of "Colter's Hell," after early explorer John Colter. He passed through the region in 1807, after separating from the Lewis and Clark Expedition.

The thermal activity results from volcanic eruptions thousands of years ago which left behind molten rock beneath the surface of the earth. Heat from this molten reservoir is close enough to the surface to cause the bubbling waters, geysers, and steam which visitors delight in viewing.

Yellowstone is also noted for its bears, which tourists are warned not to feed. But they are only one species of animal who live in this successful wildlife sanctuary, which is home to 60 varieties of mammals and 200 species of birds. Included are elk, bison, moose, mountain lion, lynx, grizzly bear, bighorn sheep, and coyote, to name only a few. Bird species include trumpeter swans, pelicans, bald eagle and osprey.

For the visitor a stop at Park Headquarters at Mammoth Hot Springs near the north entrance, or a call at one of several visitor's centers is advised. Each offers information and exhibits on the different attractions and many recreation opportunties, including over 1,000 miles of trails.

Naturally, no visit to Yellowstone is complete without a look at Old Faithful, the most renowned of the park's geysers. Since its discovery in 1870, its height, interval between spouting, and length of play have changed little. It erupts 21 to 23 times per day, discharg-

Jackson at night

ing some 5,000 to 8,000 gallons of water. The Old Faithful Visitor's center offers a geyser diagram and other displays.

Other geyser basins present good shows, too. Most of these are located in the west and south-central portions of the park. The Norris Geyser Basin, to name only one, has hundreds of geysers, pools, and thermal springs, all within a two-mile walk.

And you won't want to miss the Grand Canyon of the Yellowstone, located along the Yellowstone River between Canyon and Tower-Roosevelt, which has spectacular coloring ranging from yellow to orange to red. Artist's Point on the southern rim and Inspiration Point on the northern rim offer good vistas. For a view of the Lower Falls, try Lookout Point. A stairway dubbed Uncle Tom's Trail leads to the Falls, which are twice the height of Niagara, and descends halfway to the canyon floor.

Last in this brief introduction to the wonders of the park is Yellowstone Lake. Its 110-mile shoreline is a haven for water birds. At 7,731 feet above sea level, it is the largest body of water at so high an altitude in North America.

Regretfully we must take our leave of this popular and fascinating region. But next we'll head west to Cody and Buffalo Bill country, a land which will serve as an introduction to the northern reaches of Wyoming.

The Wild Frontier:
Northern Wyoming

Wyoming's northern reaches are, for the most part, mountainous. But throw in a few rivers, a lot of high plateau country, an abundance of Old West towns, and oh yes, some dude ranches, and you begin to get a feel for this area. Even though much of it is wilderness, it's never far from one town to the next, and all of the north country is beautiful.

Heading east from Yellowstone to Cody, we'll first drive through the spectacular high country of the Wapiti Valley in the Shoshone National Forest. Dedicated by President Benjamin Harrison in 1891, this reserve is the country's first national forest. The highway passes the Wapiti Ranger Station, which derives its name from the Indian word for elk, and was the first ranger station to be built in the United States. At two-and-a-half million acres, Shoshone is one of the country's largest national forests. It teems with an abundance of wildlife and is a major recreational area.

The first town on our northern itinerary is Cody, but no discussion of this community can begin without a word about its founder and most famous resident. Colonel William F. "Buffalo Bill" Cody has been called "the quintessential American frontiersman." He was an

Bison at the Firehole River, Yellowstone National Forest

Indian scout and Pony Express Rider who created a traveling exhibition of western life. Begun in 1883, "Buffalo Bill's Wild West Show" earned him world fame. His entourage, which included 640 cowboys, Indians, "Roughriders," musicians and technicians, and more than 400 animals, toured the United States and Europe to great acclaim. When Buffalo Bill died in 1917, more than 25,000 mourners paid their last respects.

Cody today offers many attractions, most of them linked to the town's history and famous founder. Buffalo Bill himself appears, along with his horse Smoky, in the guise of a statue in downtown Cody. Visitors to the Irma Hotel, which Colonel Cody opened in 1902, can see the $100,000 bar that was a gift from Queen Victoria to show her appreciation for the Wild West Show. The hotel has been a favorite gathering place of local cattlemen, sheepherders and oilmen for years.

The Paul Stock Center is a replica of the T.E. Ranch, Cody's beloved home which was located on the South Fork of the Shoshone River. Today it houses the town's Chamber of Commerce and an art center.

But absolutely no visit to Cody is complete without a stop at the Buffalo Bill Historical Center. The four museums which comprise the center together contain a comprehensive collection of Western Americana. At the Buffalo Bill Museum, you'll view many of his possessions and other western artifacts. The Plains Indians Museum features an extensive collection of Indian implements, representing the Sioux, Blackfeet, Cheyenne, Shoshone, Crow, and Arapaho. Artwork depicting the West is the focus of The Whitney Gallery of Western Art. And, finally, the Winchester Arms Museum has an outstanding display of the development of the firearm, with more than 5,000 items exhibited.

The restored home of early resident Caroline Lockhart is open to the public, too. The owner and editor of the Cody Enterprise lived here from 1904 to 1962. She was Boston's first woman newspaper reporter prior to her move west. (Her relocation was prompted, incidentally, by an interview with Buffalo Bill.)

To bask in more of that frontier atmosphere, tour Old Trail Town. This is a fascinating assemblage of 19th century historic buildings brought from locations elsewhere in Wyoming and reassembled on the original site of Old Cody. Among them are a log cabin hideout of Butch Cassidy and his "Wild Bunch," and a cabin used by General Custer's chief scout, "Curly." The Museum of the Old West on the town's grounds has western and Indian artifacts.

A large mineral hot springs is found at Thermopolis, southeast of Cody via Highway 120. The springs have an average temperature of 135 degrees, and are open all thanks to a treaty signed in 1897 between the Shoshone Indians and the U.S. government. At Hot Springs State Park this commitment continues to be honored, with a bath house offering both indoor and outdoor pools. The Indian's presentation of the springs to the white man is reenacted every August in the Gift of the Waters Pageant.

South of Thermopolis lies the Wind River Canyon, which the waters of the Wind River have carved more than 2,000 feet deep. Many remarkable rock formations can be seen on the canyon walls.

The town of Greybull, north of Thermopolis, takes its name from an old Indian legend. This tale told of a great albino bison bull that roamed the area which the Indians believed to be a sign from their Great Spirit. Today the community is a center for bentonite mining.

The landscape surrounding this community is rich in fossils, semi-precious stones, and Indian relics, and the Greybull Museum displays many such finds, as well as the requisite Western memorabilia.

East of Greybull we arrive at the Bighorns. All of the features which share this same name, including the mountains, the canyon, the river, the basin, the lake, the county, the town, and the forest, got their designation from the bighorn sheep. Bighorn Basin, which one crosses on the road from Cody to Greybull, is surrounded by high mountains on three

Lower Falls of Yellowstone River

Mammoth Hot Springs, Yellowstone National Park

43

sides and Montana foothills on the fourth. The basin has been likened to a "huge walled fortress"; although some simply claim it looks like a huge bowl, whose center measures roughly 70 to 90 miles across.

The Bighorn National Forest covers over one million acres, and once again the traveler faces a choice of routes. U.S. 14, east from Greybull, crosses Granite Pass at 8,950 feet and passes by Shell Canyon and Falls. The Shell Falls Overlook offers a good view of the cascading waters. An interpretive center located here explains the geology of the canyon, where Shell Creek has carved a deep granite gorge and limestone cliffs hover over all.

Up north, U.S. 14A has a different set of attractions to recommend it. The road heads east from Lovell, and passes the mysterious Medicine Wheel. This prehistoric structure is a circle of stones 245 feet in circumference with 28 spokes radiating from a cairn in the center. While nobody is certain what the purpose of this arrangement was, it is believed to have been used for celestial observations or religious ceremonies.

After traversing the Bighorns, we'll meander into Sheridan. Near the Montana border, this town lies in a region of strong English influence. In the late 19th century, British remittance men settled the area, bringing with them ranching expertise. So began the era of the cattle barons. One such cattle king home is the Bradford Brinton Memorial Ranch. Originally known as the Quarter Circle A, this site today recreates western ranch life with equipment, rare books and documents, and a collection of Western art on display.

The territory surrounding Sheridan was the scene of many major Indian battles. The Sioux, Cheyenne, and Arapaho lived here in large numbers when the white man began his settlements in the 1860's and 70's. Members of these tribes, led by such legendary warriors as Crazy Horse and Red Cloud fought to keep the steady encroachment of the white settlers at bay.

A major source of Indian anger was the Bozeman Trail. This path, a shortcut to the Montana gold fields, led directly through Indian hunting grounds. It was the scene of so many battles that it soon earned the nickname "The Bloody Bozeman." One of the worst incidents was the Fetterman Massacre, which is commemorated by a stone monument. Crazy Horse and Red Cloud ambushed William Fetterman and his party of 82 men on December 21, 1866. None of the group survived. Other Indian battles which occured in the environs were the Wagon Box Fight, the Sawyer Fight and the Connor Battle. Most are marked by posts or memorials.

Next on our journey is Buffalo, a ranching town on the eastern slope of the Bighorn Mountains. It was the spot where battles of a different sort raged — those between cattlemen and sheepherders. The short but intense Johnson County War was settled only when the U.S. Cavalry was called in. Today a large Basque contingent populates the area, descendents of sheepherders drawn to the land in the late 1800's by the location's resemblance to the Pyrennes.

At the Jim Gatchell Museum, displays detailing the history of the Buffalo area, including the Johnson County War, are shown. Gatchell was the town pharmacist who had a passion for history. He stocked his store with western relics as well as drugs, and his extensive collection formed the basis for the museum.

East by I-90 is Gillette, the Campbell County seat. First surveyed in 1891, it developed after the Burlington Railroad terminated here. This is high plateau country, and the city today is a coal mining and oil town. Several companies in the area offer coal mine tours.

Further along toward the South Dakota border is Sundance, a town which nestles at the base of a mountain known by the same name. Here the Sioux Indians held religious ceremonies and tribal councils called Wi Wacippi Paha, or Temple of the Sioux. While it is no certainty, many think that Harry Longabough of Butch Cassidy fame earned his nickname here. "The Sundance Kid" served an 18-month jail sentence for horse stealing. The Crook County Museum and Art Gallery features a display portraying the trial of Longabough.

Whitewater rafting the Snake

Grand Canyon of the Yellowstone River

Pyramid Peak in Gros Ventre Wilderness

From Sundance, let's head north to Devil's Tower National Monument. This conspicuous landmark was immortalized in celluloid by the movie, "Close Encounters of the Third Kind." The huge monolith towers nearly 1,280 feet above the valley floor and the Belle Fourche River. With its fluted, columnar sides and truncated top, some say Devil's Tower resembles a stone tree stump. Whatever it looks like, it was the country's first national monument. The Indians called the tower Mateo Tepee, meaning Bear Lodge, and it played an important role in their legends. A campground is located nearby, and naturalists conduct informational walks, campfire programs and climbing demonstrations.

Our northern Wyoming navigation ends in the Black Hills National Forest, the fabled sacred land of the Sioux Indians. Established as a national forest in 1898, the timberland extends into South Dakota and was the site of gold strikes in the 19th century. Today recreational opportunities abound.

It's been a delightful journey, but it's time to bid farewell to northern Wyoming. Next we'll drop down into the central portion of the state, and trace the route of the westward pioneers.

Rabbitbrush on Gros Ventre Range near Blue Miner Lake

Autumn on Shoshone River, Wapiti Valley

Mountain man and Crow Indian wife near Cody

Majestic Elk

Winter in Grand Teton National Park

The Snake River in spring

Fall roundup, Greybull River Valley

Wyoming sheepherder

Buffalo Bill statue, Cody

56

Old Trail Town, Cody

Island Lake, Beartooth Plateau

Brooks Lake, Bridger-Teton National Forest

Snake River and Tetons

Trumpeter Swans

Small creek in Teton Mountain range (Opposite)

Fall color on the Snake River

Grizzly Bear and cubs

The Oregon Trail:
Central Wyoming

The final leg of our journey crosses central Wyoming, following the route of the Oregon Trail, which was the emigrant's road of choice. We'll travel through wide open land, past many sites of historical interest, including museums, military posts and forts.

In its Wyoming leg, the Oregon Trail followed the North Platte and Sweetwater Rivers. Known also by such names as The California Trail, The Mormon Trail and The Platte River Road, this route was a natural to attract many travelers since it was smooth and relatively mud free. The discovery of South Pass, an easy way to cross the Rockies, guaranteed an increase in its popularity. By the peak emigration years of 1841 to 1868, it is estimated that between 350,000 and 400,000 emigrants chose this path. Their numbers were 55,000 in 1850 alone.

Modern day visitors can trace the pioneer's route beginning on U.S. 26 between Torrington and Casper. We'll start there, too, at the farming, ranching, and defense community of Torrington. Near here is the Fort Laramie National Historic Site. Situated in a fertile valley, this fort was an important fur trading center, and later a military post. It served the needs of an immense variety of people who passed by on their way west, among them gold seekers and emigrants, stage coach riders and Pony Express men.

Today the remains of the fort stand on 836 acres managed by the National Park Service. Eleven of the original structures have been restored, including Old Bedlam, the Post Trader's store, the cavalry barracks and the bachelor officer's quarters.

North of Fort Laramie is Lusk, another town located in the midst of farming and ranching activities. In the heyday of the stagecoaches, both the Cheyenne and Black Hills Stage Lines ran through the community. Exhibits from this era are displayed at the Stagecoach Museum. There's even an original stagecoach from the Cheyenne-Deadwood Line, which ran from the railhead in Cheyenne up to the Black Hills of South Dakota, where gold had been discovered. The valuable cargo of these coaches caused many daring robberies to be attempted, adding more legends to the winning of the West.

Limestone beds and prehistoric artifacts are found near Guernsey, which sits near the mouth of the Platte River Canyon. Also close at hand is the Oregon Trail Ruts State Historic Site. Here you can see grooves five to six feet deep carved into the ground by the relentless march of wagon wheels and oxen hooves. Just south of here is Register Cliff, a sandstone outcropping carved with thousands of names of pioneers.

The small community of Glendo lies northwest of Guernsey. Once the Old Horseshoe Stage Station, it is now a center for the recreational areas which surround it.

At Douglas, once called Tent Town, you'll find natives ready to show you specimens of the famous Jackalope. A huge replica of this jack rabbit — antelope hybrid stands downtown. But don't let the locals fool you — the Jackalope is really a creation of Wyoming's clever taxidermists.

Since 1905, Douglas has been the site of the Wyoming State Fair. On the fairgrounds, the Wyoming Pioneer's Memorial Museum is well worth a visit. It showcases extensive displays of pioneer artifacts. Nearby Fort Fetterman was once a major army supply post. A

Bighorn Sheep

Autumn in the Bighorn Mountains

Helen Lake in Bighorn National Forest

Cloud Peak Wilderness, Bighorn Mountains

museum displays military history.

South of Douglas lies 10,274 foot Laramie Peak. Pioneers used the mountain as a weather indicator and landmark since it can be seen for nearly a hundred miles in any direction. As the pioneers crossed into Wyoming from western Nebraska, Laramie Peak was the first mountain they saw.

Above the peak, and up north from Douglas is the Thunder Basin National Grassland, which covers two million acres. Once a useless dust bowl, the land has been rejuvenated and converted to grass where cattle, sheep, and antelope graze. Early homesteaders applied eastern farming techniques which were not well suited to these semi-arid plains. Poor soil and recurrent droughts exacerbated the problem. Thanks to wise intervention, the grassland now serves the needs of a variety of birds and wildlife.

But back to our western journey. It's on to Casper, the state's largest city. The rich oil fields of this portion of Wyoming fueled the growth of Casper. It had its first refinery, albeit a primitive one, by 1895, and recent booms in uranium, coal and oil production have added more prosperity to the area. Today nearly 400 oil company affiliates have offices in Casper.

It seems Casper's residents have always had a knack for capitalizing on opportunity, for here was the scene where a group of Mormon emigrants in 1847 realized that boating travelers across the North Platte River could earn them money. The ferry they operated became a toll bridge in the 1850's. Soon a fort was built to protect the bridge and those who travelled across it. Fort Caspar, three miles west of the city, is a replica of this historic outpost. An interpretive building is featured.

Both the fort and the city were named for Lieutenant Caspar Collins, who died while trying to rescue a wagon train from Indians in 1865. Though the fort maintains the original spelling of the poor lieutenant's name, a spelling error somewhere along the line caused the city to be dubbed Casper with an "e."

Also worth a visit in town is the Natrona County Pioneer Museum, which exhibits photos and artifacts. It is inside Casper's first church, built in 1891. At the Werner Wildlife Museum you'll see animal displays and an antelope diorama. Casper Mountain lies south of the city, and the view from its peak is amazing. The surrounding recreation zone is used for camping, hiking, and picnicking.

Those keen on political history may want to make the 35-mile drive north of Casper to view Teapot Rock. Though a violent windstorm damaged the formation in 1962 and it no longer quite so closely resembles a teapot as it once did, here was the site from which one of America's famous political scandals derived its name.

The rich Teapot Dome oil fields which encompass the rock were leased in secret with no bidding allowed by the government. U.S. Senate hearings ensued, and when they revealed that the fields had been leased to the Mammoth Oil Company, the attendant uproar resulted in prison terms for Secretary of the Interior Albert B. Fall and oil company owner Harry F. Sinclair.

Returning from this side trip, we'll follow the Sweetwater River southwest to the Independence Rock State Historic Site. This isolated granite boulder is the most well-known of all the places where pioneers carved their names. Father DeSmet named it "The Great Register of the Desert." (He added his own name in 1840.) Emigrants compared the 193-foot rock to "a great turtle," "a bowl turned upside down" or "a huge whale." No matter what they thought it looked like, more than 5,000 of them carved their names on it. A favorite rest stop on the Oregon Trail, Independence Rock was named July 4, 1830 by a group of fur traders led by William Sublette.

Just a bit west of Independence Rock, another landmark duly noted by the pioneers in their journals is Devil's Gate, a canyon through which the Sweetwater River flows. Just 400 yards long, the chasm narrows to a width of 35 feet at its eastern end, leaving barely enough room for the river to pass through.

Ayers Natural Bridge, Casper

Thunderhead over Buffalo

The western wayfarers arrived at South Pass 60 miles later. Many were disappointed that the Continental Divide crossing was barely noticeable. Close by, South Pass City boomed when gold was found in the area, and 4,000 people lived here by 1871. One of them was Esther Hobart Morris, who persuaded territorial legislators to pass the first woman's suffrage law in the nation.

Alas, the boom in South Pass City was not to last, and by 1875 it was deserted, with many of its buildings moved to Lander. But, the town lives on as the South Pass City State Historic Site, with many of its ghost town buildings undergoing renovation, and living history programs offered in summer.

Lander, to the north, is one of Wyoming's oldest communities. It started as a surveyor's post called Camp McGraw in 1857-58. Indian unrest proved to be a continuing problem in the territory until 1872, when the United States government transferred many natives to Idaho, and officially opened the region to settlement. In 1884, Lander became the seat of Fremont County, which, at 5,861,200 acres, is as large as some eastern states.

Land which was once part of a horse ranch operated by George Parker lies within the county's borders. (You probably know Parker better by his nickname, Butch Cassidy.) Where outlaws once roamed, now sits the Wind River Indian Reservation.

It is home to over 4,000 members of the Shoshone and Arapaho tribes. Because they are of different linguistic stock and cultural heritage, there is little intermixing of the two. The Shoshones live in the south-central, western, and northern sections of the reservation, while the Arapaho inhabit the southeastern corner.

It was in 1868 that U.S. treaty makers at Fort Bridger came to an agreement with Chief Washakie that most of current-day Fremont County be deeded to the Shoshones for their permanent home. Today, the reservation covers 2,250,000 acres of land. Buried within its boundaries are Chief Washakie, the first Indian to be buried with military honors, and Sacajawea, the famous Shoshone who guided Lewis and Clark. Today, oil and gas leases account for much of the tribe's income, but farming and ranching is also prevalent on the reservation.

Many special events are held here, including the Sun Dances performed at Ethete and Fort Washakie, Christmas holiday dances, and the Arapaho Powwow in August.

It seems fitting to end our journey through Wyoming where the state's history began thousands of years ago — among the native American Indians. Their legacy mixes with that of the white men who settled here to create a richly textured history for this western state.

The story continues to be written today, as Wyoming assumes its place as one of the great energy-producing areas of the world, and emigrants drawn by these riches are still lured west.

But our part in this epic adventure must end here. Whether you have the good fortune to visit the state of Wyoming, or must admire it from afar, hopefully the tale told within these pages has convinced you that Wyoming is indeed a state to be admired.

Devil's Tower

Hell's Half Acre (Opposite)

Pronghorn Antelope

Photo Credits

A word about our author:
Charlotte Dixon

We couldn't have picked a better person to do the text for this book than our author, Charlotte Dixon. A free-lance journalist living in Portland, Oregon, her great-great grandparents were among the hardy pioneers who followed the Oregon Trail across Wyoming to settle in the West. She has had an affinity for the area all of her life.

With her heritage and extensive travelling in the state she has been able to impart that very important "first hand" knowledge that make her writings so enjoyable.

She has a degree in journalism from the University of Oregon and she is a past president of the Willamette Writers Association. She is kept busy contributing essays and profiles to a variety of local magazines and newspapers, while she continues to work actively to promote the literary arts in the Northwest.

Her association with Beautiful America Publishing Company began when she wrote the text for, *Beautiful America's MAINE.*

When she isn't busy at her hobbies of gardening, knitting, reading and hiking, she is travelling continually with her husband and two children throughout the West and especially Wyoming.

Medicine Bow National Forest

(Rear Cover) Moss Campion